COMPARING
RELIGIONS

Pilgrimages and Journeys

Katherine Prior

Thomson Learning
New York

Comparing Religions

Birth Customs
Death Customs
Food and Fasting
Initiation Customs
Marriage Customs
Pilgrimages and Journeys

About this book

This book looks at the very old custom of pilgrimage as it is practiced in six of the world's major religions. Pilgrimage is an important part of religious life because it is a form of worship that everyone can take part in regardless of wealth or education.

Each chapter compares the approaches of different religions to one aspect of religious journeying. The book looks at why people go on pilgrimages, where they go, how they behave and dress on the journey, and what they do at their destination. It also describes some pilgrimages and pilgrims from the past and explains some of the interaction between different religions.

---

3 9082 05341784 9

First published in the
United States in 1993 by
Thomson Learning
115 Fifth Avenue
New York, NY 10003

First published in 1992 by
Wayland (Publishers) Ltd

Cataloging-in-Publication Data applied for

ISBN: 1-56847-032-0

Printed in Italy

Contents

Introduction   4
What is a holy site?   5
Pilgrimages in the past   12
Why do people go on pilgrimages today? 16
The journey   20
Dressing and behaving like a pilgrim   22
Worshiping at the holy site   24
The way home   29
Glossary   30
Books to read   31
Index   32

Words that appear in **bold** in the text are
explained in the glossary on page 30.

Introduction

A pilgrimage is a religious journey, and the people who go on pilgrimages are called pilgrims. They are not like business travelers or tourists on vacation. They travel to places that are considered holy in their religion because they want to become closer to their god.

Pilgrimage is a very popular form of **worship.** Every year, millions of pilgrims from many different religions make special religious journeys. Anyone can be a pilgrim, whether rich or poor, male or female, old or young.

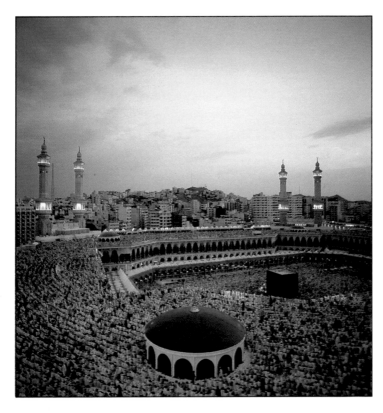

Left Huge numbers of Muslims go on a pilgrimage to Mecca for the Hajj every year.

What is a holy site?

A holy site is a place where people go to feel very close to their god and their religion. Every religion has places that are special to it. Some are very busy and are in the center of big, bustling cities. Pilgrims can get to these places in airplanes, trains, and cars. But some holy sites are high up in snow-covered mountains, and pilgrims have to climb up the slippery slopes on foot or ride on the backs of donkeys.

Below The Hindu god, Rama, was born in Ayodhya in northern India. This is one of many temples there dedicated to Rama.

In India, Hindus have many holy sites that are linked to stories of how their gods and goddesses came down from heaven to live on earth. Wherever a god was born or lived became a holy place. Today Hindus go on pilgrimages to these places because they hope to see the spot where a god traveled between heaven and earth. Hindus who worship the god Rama go on pilgrimages to his birthplace in Ayodhya in northern India. Hindus who worship the god Krishna make pilgrimages to the towns of Brindaban and Mathura, where Krishna was born and grew up.

Buddhists have holy sites in India, too. These sites show where important things happened in the life of the Buddha. The Buddha was a prince who lived in India about 2,500 years ago. Buddhists do not worship him as a god, but they know that he lived a very holy life and learned the secret of living in perfect peace.

At Buddh Gaya pilgrims can see the holy tree where the Buddha sat and prayed for a long time. Here he learned how to live without selfishness or greed. The tree he sat under is called the Tree of Enlightenment. At Sarnath they can see where the Buddha began to teach his **disciples** the first lessons of Buddhism. Pilgrims go to these holy sites today to understand more about the Buddha's teaching.

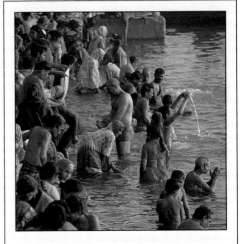

Varanasi is a holy site for Hindus because it is on the bank of the holy river Ganges. Radhika was ten years old when she visited Varanasi with her parents:

"Early on our first morning we climbed down the steps to take a bath in the Ganges. It was still almost dark and the water was very cold! A priest helped us say our prayers and I lit a small flaoting candle as an offering to the Goddess of the Ganges."

Right An important holy site for Buddhists is this tree in Buddh Gaya, India. It is known as the Tree of Enlightenment, and Buddhists believe this is where the Buddha learned how to live in perfect peace.

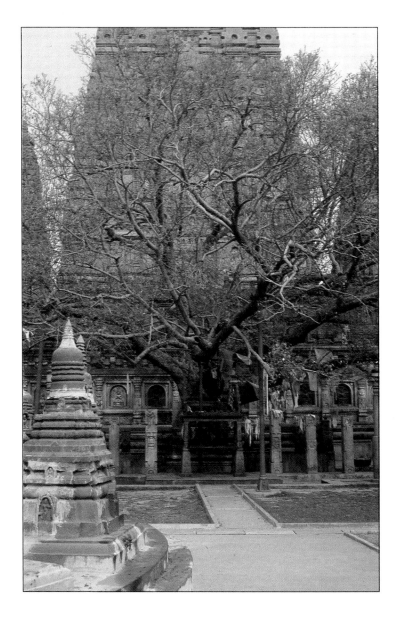

The whole of Israel is special to Jews. Thousands of years ago, God promised them that they would always be able to feel his presence in Jerusalem. To give thanks to God for this promise, King Solomon had a magnificent temple of stone built in the city. Jewish men made three pilgrimages a year to the temple until it was almost completely

7

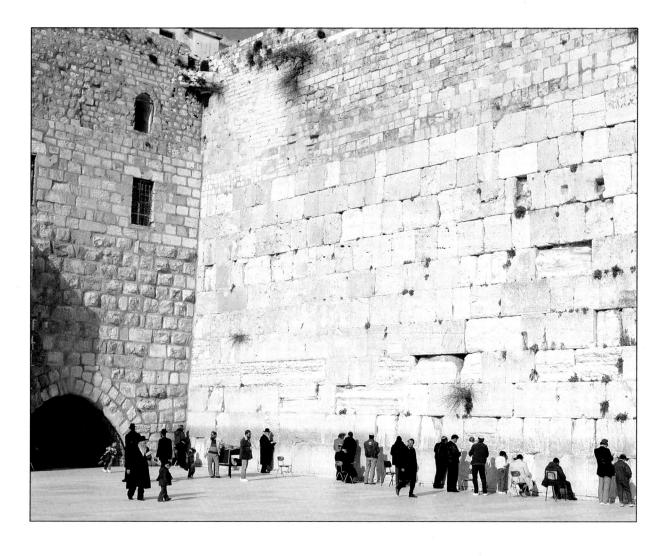

destroyed by the Romans in A.D. 70. Today, only a single wall is left. This is called the Western Wall, and Jews come from all over the world to pray here and feel close to God.

Christians regard all of Israel, where Jesus lived and taught, as the Holy Land, but the most important sites are in Jerusalem, where Jesus died and came back to life. Jesus was born almost 1,000 years after Solomon had built the Temple of the Jews. Christians believe

Above The Western Wall in Jerusalem is all that remains of the Jewish temple first built there by King Solomon nearly 3,000 years ago.

that Jesus was the son of God, and that God sent him to earth to show people how to worship the one God and obtain **eternal** life. But Jesus's teaching upset the Jewish leaders and Roman rulers of Jerusalem. He was put to death at the time of year now called Easter. Every Easter, pilgrims gather at the hill of Calvary where he was **crucified** and thank God for sending Jesus to teach them about Christianity.

Muslims go on pilgrimages to places that were important in the life of the

Below The great courtyard of the Sacred Mosque at Mecca can hold up to 500,000 pilgrims. At prayer times, everyone kneels on prayer mats facing the Kaaba in the center.

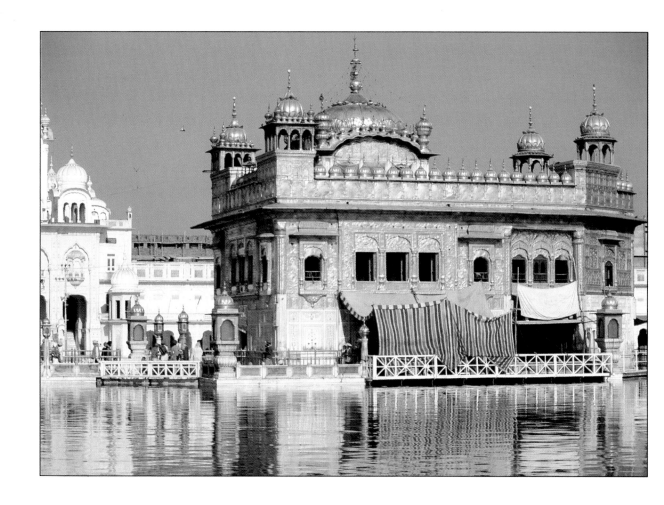

prophet Muhammad. Muhammad was born almost 1,500 years ago. Muslims believe that he was the holy messenger of Allah and was sent to earth to teach people to worship only one god. Allah is the Muslim name for God.

The city of Mecca in Saudi Arabia is the most important holy site for Muslims. Here, in an ancient building called the Kaaba, or God's House, Muhammad stopped his countrymen from praying to **idols**, or statues of different gods, and showed them how to worship the one God, or Allah. Every

Above The beautiful Golden Temple in Amristar, India, is the holiest center for Sikhs.

year, millions of Muslims come to Mecca to worship Allah.

Sikhs have many holy sites associated with the lives of their ten **gurus**, or holy teachers. The most sacred is the Golden Temple in the city of Amristar in India. The temple looks like a golden island floating in the middle of a large lake. The tenth guru was Govind Singh, and he instructed all of his followers to come and bathe in the holy waters that surround the Golden Temple.

Martyrs

Every religion has good teachers and leaders. Sometimes these holy men and women let themselves be killed by their enemies rather than give up their religious beliefs. People who do this are called martyrs. They show that they love their god more than they love their own life. When a holy person is martyred, people will often go on a pilgrimage to the place where he or she is buried.

One of the most famous Sikh martyrs was the ninth guru, Tegh Bahadur. He was beheaded 300 years ago on the orders of the Mogul emperor. A Sikh temple, the Gurdwara Rakab Ganj, was built at the place in Delhi, India, where Tegh Bahadur's body was **cremated**. Every year, thousands of Sikhs make pilgrimages there to honor the sacrifice he made for his religion.

Below Sikhs gather at the Gurdwara Rakab Ganj to remember the life of the ninth guru, Tegh Bahadur.

Pilgrimages in the past

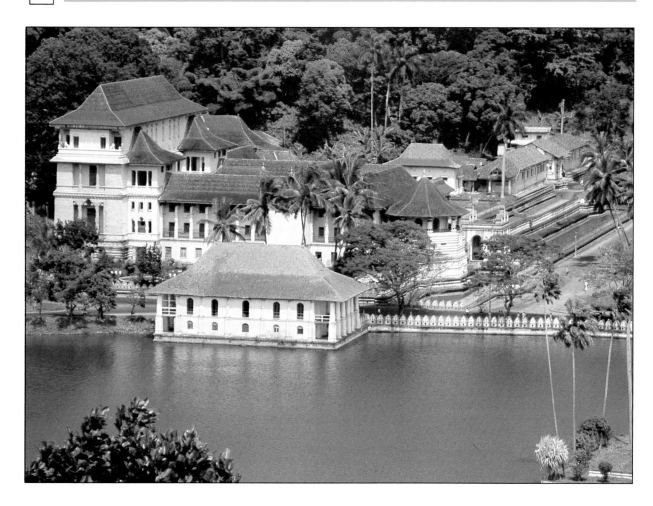

Most religions are very old, and many have grown and changed a lot since their beginnings. Some religions have spread a long way from the countries where they started. New holy sites appeared wherever the religion went, at places where a holy person died or was buried or where a miracle occurred.

Buddhism spread from India to Sri Lanka, Burma, Thailand, Nepal, Tibet,

Above   The Temple of the Tooth in Sri Lanka contains a tooth that is said to have been one of the Buddha's. Many pilgrims visit places that are believed to contain **relics** from religious leaders.

China, and Japan. All of these countries have holy sites associated with the teachers who first brought Buddhism to them. There are also holy sites that pilgrims visit where relics, or remains, of the Buddha are kept. A famous temple in the town of Kandy in Sri Lanka preserves a tooth said to have been one of the Buddha's.

After the death of Jesus, Christianity spread to Europe and then to the Americas. In 1531, at Guadalupe in Mexico, a poor man had a **vision** of the Virgin Mary, the mother of Jesus Christ.

Below Roman Catholics worship at a shrine to the Virgin Mary in Guadalupe, Mexico. A special service is held there every year to celebrate the appearance of the Virgin Mary to a local man.

She told him to build a **shrine** in her name at Guadalupe and, ever since, thousands of Roman Catholics from all parts of Latin America have traveled there each year on December 12 to celebrate Our Lady of Guadalupe Day.

Islam spread very widely from its beginnings in Arabia. In Asia and Africa, many Muslims go on pilgrimages to the tombs of the holy teachers who brought Islam to their countries.

Battles over holy sites

All religions teach people to be good and kind, but members of different religions often fight one another because they want to prove that their religion is the right one and that their idea of God is the best one. Some people will go to war if their holy sites are controlled by members of a different religion.

Judiasm, Christianity, and Islam all began in the countries bordering the Red Sea in the area that we now call the Middle East. The three religions have many holy sites that are very close together, and Jews, Christians, and Muslims have fought many battles over these holy sites.

The biggest battles of all were the Crusades in the **Middle Ages**. Thousands of Christians marched from Europe to the land where Jesus had lived to fight Muslims who were living there.

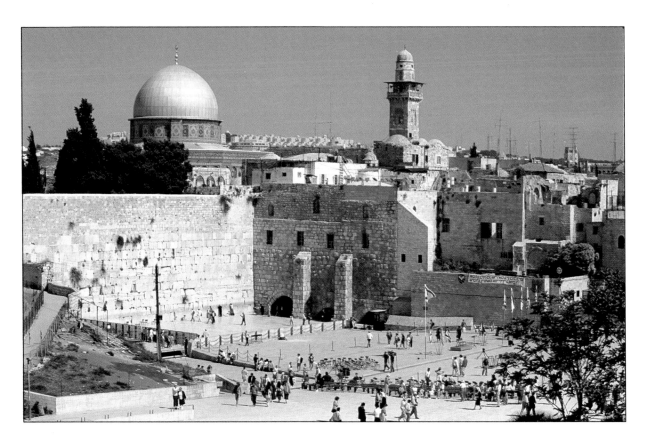

Above In Jerusalem, Muslims and Jews worship very close to each other. Here you can see that the Muslim Dome of the Rock overlooks the Jewish Western Wall.

Today, although Jerusalem is controlled by the Jewish state of Israel, there are still problems with its holy sites. Hundreds of years ago, the Muslims built a beautiful **mausoleum** on the site of the old Temple of the Jews. It is called the Dome of the Rock, and it marks the place where Muhammad rode up to heaven on his sacred horse. For Muslims, it is a very holy site, but it is also a holy site for Jews because the Western Wall is nearby.

In India, there are holy sites that are claimed by both Hindus and Muslims. Muslim invaders sometimes destroyed Hindu temples and built mosques on the temple ruins.

15

Why do people go on pilgrimages today?

People go on pilgrimages for many different reasons, but all pilgrims hope that they will feel closer to their god by visiting a holy site.

Giving thanks and asking for favors
Sometimes people go on pilgrimages when something special has happened to them. A sick person who gets better or a person who has had good fortune may go on a pilgrimage to give thanks for their happiness.

Some people go on pilgrimages to ask their god for a favor. Perhaps they want a new business to be successful, or their children to pass their exams in school, or rain to fall and make their crops grow. They **vow** to make another pilgrimage if their prayers are answered.

Praying for good health
Every religion has holy sites where pilgrims who are sick pray to be made healthy. They have illnesses their doctors cannot cure, so they ask their god to make them better.

At Lourdes in France there is a spring of water which is believed to have

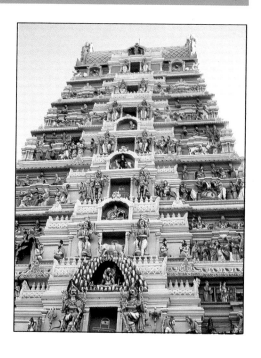

Above The temples at Hindu holy sites often display beautiful carvings like these.

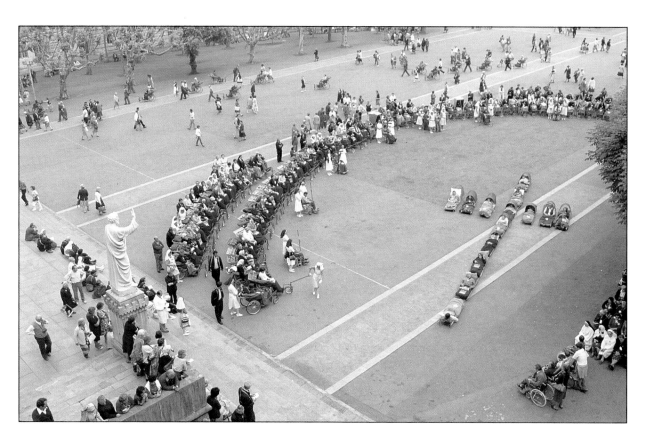

healing powers. It became famous about 150 years ago, when the Virgin Mary appeared in a vision to a peasant girl and showed her where the spring was. Today, Roman Catholics who are ill go to Lourdes from all over Europe to bathe in the springwater and to pray to the Virgin Mary to be cured.

In India there is a very old tree growing by the sacred tank of the Sikh Golden Temple. Four hundred years ago, a **leper** took a bath in the pond near the tree and was miraculously cured of his disease. Since then, many Sikhs have bathed at this spot in the hope that they will be cured of their illnesses.

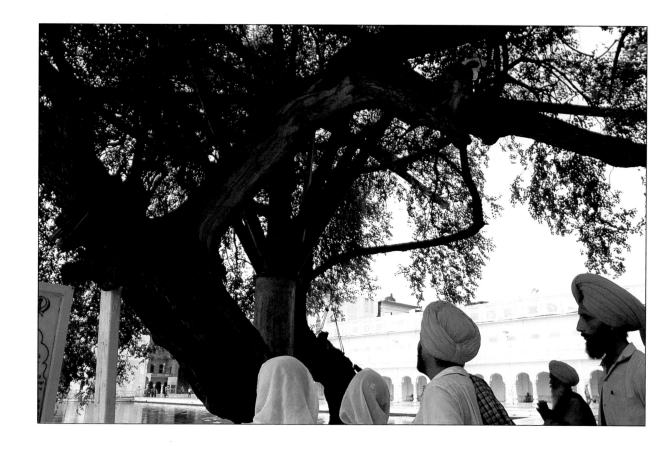

Even healthy pilgrims often bathe at holy sites. This is because many religions use water as a **symbol**, or sign, of purity. When pilgrims take a bath, it is a way of showing that they are washing their hearts and minds clean of any bad thoughts.

Above Sikhs believe that this tree growing beside the Golden Temple in Amristar has special healing powers. Sikhs who are ill hope to be cured by bathing in the water around the tree.

Coming together

In Islam, pilgrimage is required. Every adult Muslim who can afford it and who is healthy must go on a pilgrimage to Mecca at least once in his or her lifetime. This pilgrimage is called the Hajj, and it only happens for a few days each year in Dhu al-Hijjah, the twelfth month of the

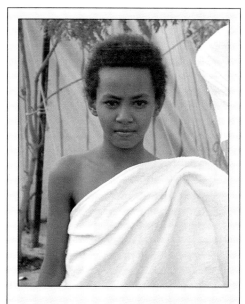

Ali was 12 when he and his father traveled from Indonesia for the Hajj:

"It was wonderful, but a little frightening, to see all those thousands and thousands of people from so many different places. We had a guide who explained things to us because we couldn't understand the language. But even though people looked different and spoke other languages, we were still all Muslims and we all said the same prayers and did the same things. I was really proud to be a Muslim when I saw everyone praying together."

Islamic calendar. The Hajj brings millions of Muslims together from all around the world and shows them that they belong to one enormous family.

In Judaism, pilgrimage also brings people together. There is no special time for making a pilgrimage to the Western Wall in Jerusalem, but even if a Jew visits the wall alone she or he will still get a very precious feeling of belonging to a large religious family. The Western Wall holds a lot of Jewish history, and making a pilgrimage there is like having a magical meeting with all the Jews of the past.

Below Ritual bathing is an important part of many religions. Hindus bathe in the Ganges River because they believe its water is holy.

The journey

The journey to the holy site is a very important part of a pilgrimage. Before modern transportation, it was often very hard to get to a holy site, but most pilgrims did not complain about how difficult it was because they were happy to be making the pilgrimage.

Today, some pilgrims travel in such comfort that they look like ordinary tourists. Jews, Christians, and Muslims can fly to the Middle East from almost anywhere in the world. Hindus, Sikhs, and Buddhists can join pilgrimage bus tours in India that take them to several of their holy sites in just a few days. Christains can catch special pilgrimage trains to Lourdes in France; prayers and hymns are broadcast throughout the train, and there are special ambulance cars for the sick pilgrims. Many governments and religious organizations spend a lot of money making the journey comfortable for pilgrims.

Even today, however, some pilgrims do not take the easy way to get to their holy site. They are prepared to give up a lot of their time and all the comforts of modern travel to show how much they love their god. Some Christian pilgrims still walk across northern Spain to the

Below Pilgrims sometimes suffer for their religion. By walking barefoot in snow to a holy site, this pilgrim is showing that he can put up with pain for his god.

Right Inside the cathedral at Santiago de Compostela in Spain, Christian pilgrims hug a statue of St. James, an early Christian martyr.

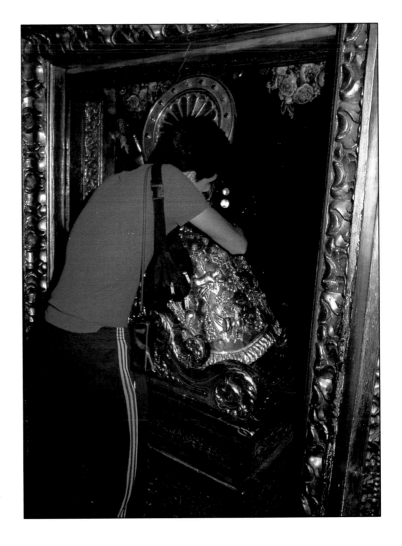

tomb of St. James, an early Christian martyr, at Santiago de Compostela. This is called the Way of St. James. Some Hindu pilgrims walk barefoot all the way to their holy sites to show that they are prepared to put up with pain for their god. Occasionally, some Buddhist and Hindu pilgrims will even cover long distances by crawling on their hands and knees. The pilgrims' desire to serve their religion is shown by their willingness to suffer for it.

Dressing and behaving like a pilgrim

Pilgrims need to prepare themselves for their journey and show that they are really thinking about their religious duties while they are traveling. They often wear special clothes so that on their journey other people will recognize them as pilgrims and will treat them with kindness and respect.

Below Buddhist monks in Thailand are easy to recognize in their orange robes.

Hindus have a holy bath at home and say special prayers with their family priest before they begin a pilgrimage. For the entire journey they try to think pure thoughts and not get angry or shout at any person or animal. Their clothes are often white or saffron, a deep yellow color. These are the colors that Hindus wear to show that they are not interested in the everyday things going on around them and that they are only interested in thinking about their God.

Many Buddhist pilgrims, especially monks, wear saffron-colored robes. Buddhist pilgrims must remember to treat the Buddha and other holy teachers with respect. They try not to laugh or be too lighthearted when they are visiting holy sites.

Above A Muslim family prepares for the Hajj. They are all dressed in the special clothes for pilgrims called *ihram.*

Among Christians, Roman Catholics confess their **sins** to their priest before they set out on a pilgrimage. This helps them to travel with only goodness in their hearts. Many Christian pilgrims do not look very different from ordinary travelers, although they often wear a badge to show where they are going. Pilgrims going to Santiago de Compostela wear a cockle shell, which shows that their holy site is by the sea. Pilgrims in the Middle Ages also used the shell as a spoon or food scoop.

Muslims going on the Hajj have a special type of dress called *ihram,* which they put on before they reach Mecca. For men, this is two pieces of plain white cotton cloth. One is folded around the waist, and the other hangs over the left shoulder. Muslim women wear a long white cotton dress. Before they put on *ihram* the pilgrims take a **purifying** bath and annouce their intention of performing the Hajj.

As long as they are wearing *ihram,* the pilgrims must not tell lies or get angry. They must not wear perfume, makeup, or jewelry. They must not look at themselves in mirrors. If they did any of these things, it would show that they were more concerned about themselves than about Allah. The pilgrims must show that they are thinking about Allah all the time.

Worshiping at the holy site

Pilgrims often have special things to do at their holy site to make sure that their pilgrimage is a successful one and that their god has heard their prayers.

For Jews, a pilgrimage to the Western Wall is a solemn occasion because the wall reminds them of the destruction of the Temple. On a special date, 9 Av in the Jewish calendar, the anniversary of the Temple's destruction, many pilgrims gather at the wall to mourn their loss. The pilgrims used to cry so loudly on this sad anniversary that non-Jewish

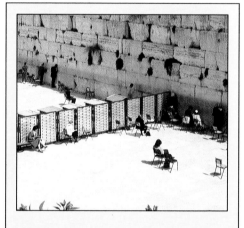

Rachel, an American girl who went to the Western Wall, said:
"Some of my friends at home think it is funny that we keep the men and the women apart, but we have to concentrate on praying. We shouldn't be trying to see what the boys on the other side of the fence look like."

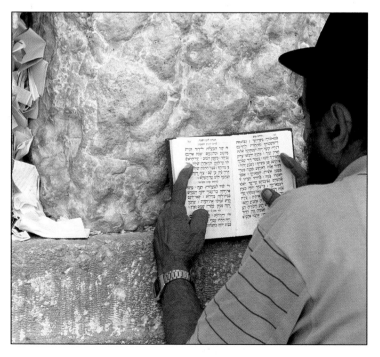

Left Jewish pilgrims at the Western Wall sometimes write their prayers on pieces of paper and push them between the stones of the wall.

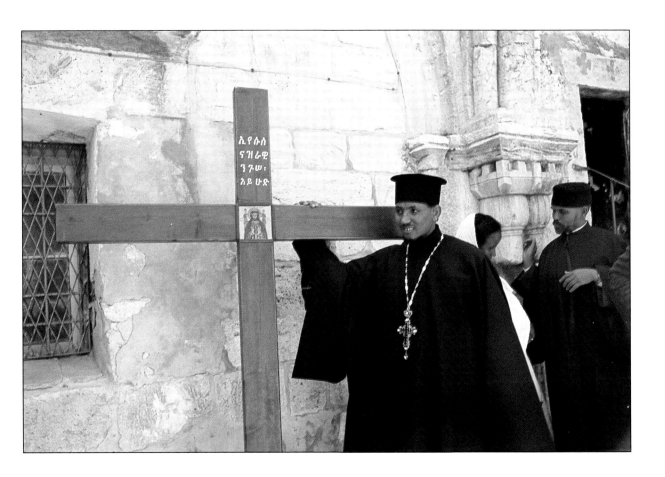

Above Jerusalem is also important to Christians. On Good Friday, the day Jesus died, Christians walk through the streets of the city. Jesus was forced to walk through Jerusalem carrying the cross on which he would later die.

people called it the "Wailing Wall." As with any public gathering of **Orthodox Jews**, men and women are separated by a curtain at the Wall.

In Jerusalem during Easter Week, Roman Catholic and **Orthodox Christians** follow the last movements Jesus made in the days before he was crucified and died on Good Friday. On these days, the pilgrims are sorrowful. They do not wear bright clothes, and many of them either **fast** or eat only a little food. On Easter Sunday, the day they believe Jesus came back to life, the pilgrims are joyful and sing hymns praising God for his power and goodness. They celebrate by eating rich food and wearing their best clothes.

The Hajj is a complicated pilgrimage, and many Muslims hire guides who tell them what to do on each day of their visit to Mecca. An important part of the Hajj is called the "standing." Pilgrims stand all day on the Mount of Mercy at Arafat to remember that this is where Muhammad gave his farewell sermon on his own pilgrimage. Near the end of the Hajj, the pilgrims kill a goat or sheep in **sacrifice**. This shows that they are willing to give something up to Allah

Below A traditional form of Hindu worship is *puja*, when an offering is made before a sacred fire. This family is burning candles in front of the image of a Hindu god.

Above These Buddhist women in Tibet are lying face down before an image of the Buddha. This shows that they are humble while they worship.

and reminds them to be **charitable**. They must give a portion of the meat to the poor.

When Hindu pilgrims reach their holy sites, they bathe in a river or tank and pray for their sins to be washed away. A priest will often say the prayers for them. After bathing, the pilgrims have their heads shaved, although most women just have one or two locks of their hair cut off. At large Hindu festivals, the government has trouble getting rid of the mountains of hair!

When their bodies and hearts are properly cleansed, the pilgrims are ready to face their god in a temple. They will pray before him or her and give little gifts of money, flowers, and candles. Some holy sites have many temples with many gods and goddesses. A pilgrim can be busy for several days going to see all of them.

At Buddhist holy sites, the pilgrims show respect to the Buddha and other great teachers by bowing or lying facedown on the ground before images of these teachers. This is called prostration. It is a way for the pilgrims to show that they are unimportant before the wisdom of their teachers.

Every Sikh holy site has a temple called a *gurdwara* that contains a copy of the Guru Granth Sahib, the holy book of the Sikhs. Sikhs bow down before the book as a way of showing it respect. The Sikhs were taught by the gurus to be charitable and to treat all people as equals. At holy sites, they follow these principles by opening kitchens that give free food to anyone who comes. The kitchens are called *langars*. The food is usually vegetarian (without meat), and everyone sits on the floor and eats together. Pilgrims often do a good deed while they are at a holy site. They may help serve the food in the *langar* or they may sweep the floors.

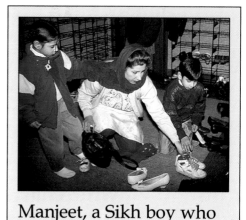

Manjeet, a Sikh boy who has been to the Golden Temple, said:
"We take our shoes off before we go into a *gurdwara*. At the Golden Temple, I cleaned some of the other pilgrims' shoes. Some of them were really dusty and a little smelly! But it is important that we do jobs like that. We have to remember that God likes even simple work and that no one is too important to work for God."

The way home

Many pilgrims like to take something back to their homes to remind them of their pilgrimage. This is often some earth or water that they have collected from the holy site and which they keep for the rest of their lives.

A pilgrim returning home is someone special. Hindu pilgrims receive a warm welcome from their family and friends. They often have a feast, and everybody eats sweets brought back from the holy site. Bottles containing water from the Ganges may be placed in home shrines. Christian pilgrims are sometimes asked to tell the people in their local churches about their experiences. Muslims who have returned from the Hajj are given the title Hajji. This way even strangers will know that they have been to Mecca.

Right Visitors to the holy spring at Lourdes may collect some of the water and take it home with them.

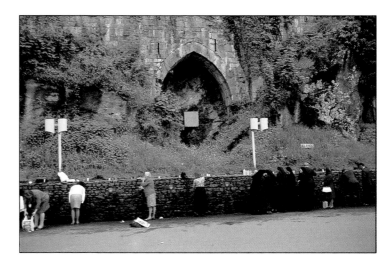

Glossary

Charitable Kind and generous to others.

Cremate To burn a dead body.

Crucify To put to death by nailing or binding the hands and feet to a cross.

Disciple A follower of a religious leader.

Eternal Lasting forever.

Fast To go without food.

Gurus Hindu or Sikh religious leaders and teachers.

Idol A statue of a god.

Leper Someone who suffers from leprosy, a disease that results in loss of feeling and decay in body parts.

Mausoleum A large elaborate tomb.

Middle Ages The period in European history from 500 to 1500.

Orthodox Christians Members of a division of Christianity that is strong in Eastern Europe and Russia.

Orthodox Jews Members of the division of Judaism that strictly follows the teachings of Moses.

Purify To cleanse thoroughly.

Relics The remains of a holy person's body and his or her possessions.

Sacrifice To make an offering to, or give up something for, a god.

Shrine A sacred place in which the holy relics of a saint are kept.

Sins Negative thoughts and actions.

Symbol A sign that stands for something that is hard to explain in ordinary words.

Vision The magical, dreamlike appearance of a god or saint.

Vow A solemn promise.

Worship To show devotion and respect to God.

Books to read

Barbarians, Christians, and Muslims (Minneapolis: Lerner Publications, 1975)

Buddhist Festivals (Vero Beach, Fl.: Rourke Corp., 1987)

Christian Celebrations for Autumn & Winter (Carthage, Ill.: Good Apple, 1990)

Jewish Days and Holidays (Bellmore, N.Y.: Adama Publications, 1986)

Many Children: Religions Around the World (Reston, Va.: M.A. Thomas, 1987)

Religion and Society (Milwaukee: Gareth Stevens Inc., 1991)

Sikh Festivals (Vero Beach, Fl.: Rourke Corp., 1993)

Picture acknowledgments

The publishers wish to thank the following for supplying the photographs in this book:
J. Allan Cash 8, 10, 12, 16, 19 (right), 24 (both), 25, 26; Cephas Picture Library 29 (Frank B. Higham); David Cumming 21; Eye Ubiquitous 19 (left, Peter Sanders), 27 (Julia Waterlow); D. Henderson 18; Hutchison Library 7 (J. Pate), 13 (Liba Taylor), 17 (Bernard Régent), 20 (Dave Brinicombe), 23 (Bernard Gerard); Christine Osborne Pictures 28; Ann & Bury Peerless 5, 11; Tony Stone Worldwide (Nabeel Turner), 9 (Nabeel Turner), 15 (Hugh Sitton), 22; Zefa, cover.

Index

Numbers in **bold** indicate photographs

Buddha, The 6, 13, 28
Buddhist monks 22, 28

Delhi 11
Dome of the Rock 15, **15**

Easter Sunday 25

Golden Temple **10**, 11, 17, **18**,
  28
Guadalupe **13**, 13–14
gurdwaras **11**, 11, 28
Guru Granth Sahib 28
Gurus
    Govind Singh 11
    Tegh Bahadur 11

Hajj 18–19, 23, 26, 29
Hindu deities
    Krishna 6
    Rama 6
holy bathing 11, 17, 18, **19**, 22,
  23, 27

ihram, 23, **23**

Jerusalem 7–9, 14–15, 19, 25
Jesus Christ 8–9, 13, 25

Kaaba 10

Lourdes 16–17, **17**, 20, **29**

martyrs 11
Mecca **4**, **9**, 10, 18, **19**, 23, 26
Muhammad 10, 15

Orthodox Christians 25

prostration **27**, 28

Roman Catholics 14, 23, 25

Santiago de Compostela 21,
  21, 23
sick pilgrims 16–17

Temple of the Tooth **12**, 13
Tree of Enlightenment 6, **7**

Virgin Mary 13, 17
visions 13, 17

Western Wall **8**, 8, 15, 19, 24,
  24